Moms are
Angels

by Bonnie Altenhein
Illustrations by Monica Sheehan

WINGS BOOKS
New York • Avenel, New Jersey

This 1995 edition is published by Wings Books,
distributed by Random House Value Publishing, Inc.,
40 Engelhard Avenue, Avenel, New Jersey 07001,
by arrangement with the author.

Random House
New York • Toronto • London • Sydney • Auckland

Printed and bound in the United States of America

Library of Congress Cataloging-in-Publication Data

Altenhein, Bonnie.
    Moms are angels / by Bonnie Altenhein; illustrations by Monica
Sheehan.
        p.   cm.
    ISBN 0-517-12241-3
    1. Mothers—Quotations, maxims, etc.   2. Mothers—Caricatures and
cartoons.   3. Angels—Quotations, maxims, etc.   4. Angels—Caricatures
and cartoons.   5. American wit and humor, Pictorial.   I. Sheehan,
Monica.   II. .Title.
PN6084.M6A47   1995
741.5'973—dc20   94-43905
                                                               CIP

8 7 6 5 4 3 2 1

To everyone's mom,
especially my mother Pauline,
Aunt Adele, Grandma Gussie, Mary,
Mary Jane, and Dorothy.

Special Dedication
To Rose, Grace, Maureen, Denise,
Trixie, and all the moms loving
children with special needs.
You are truly angels on earth.
—B.A.

Even an angel needs a vacation once in a while, or at least a ten-minute break for a cappuccino! Moms were created as back-ups for the angels, so someone is always watching over us wherever we go. As specially appointed stand-ins for our personal guardian angels, moms are well-trained to expertly handle all of our "angel-ing" needs, from bringing us hot chocolate when we're feeling blue to believing in the magic of our dreams...from laughing at our jokes to wiping away our tears. Moms can mend our teddy bears, prom dresses, and broken hearts. They are with us in good times and in sad, when we are little children or all grown up—but feeling like a child. Moms are with us on earth for a while, and in our hearts and spirits forever.

Moms are angels who share your dreams and believe they will come true.

Angels can't be everywhere.
That's why God created mothers.

Mother knows best.

Moms are angels who always know the answers to "Why?" and "How come?"

All mothers are working mothers.

Moms are special angels who only do it for your own good.

Moms are special angels who are sometimes dads.

Moms are special angels who make you practice the piano so you won't be sorry later.

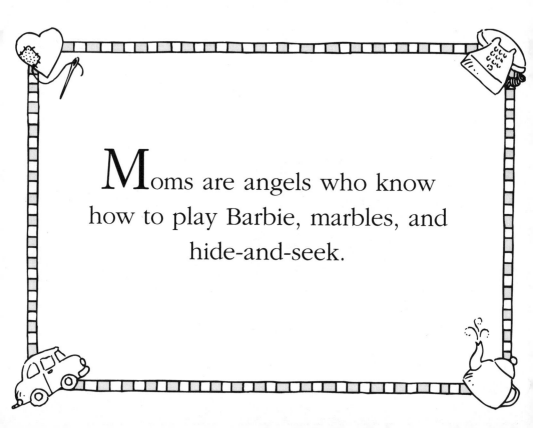

Moms are angels who know how to play Barbie, marbles, and hide-and-seek.

Moms hide silly love notes
inside your lunch box.

A rich child is often cuddled in a poor mother's lap.

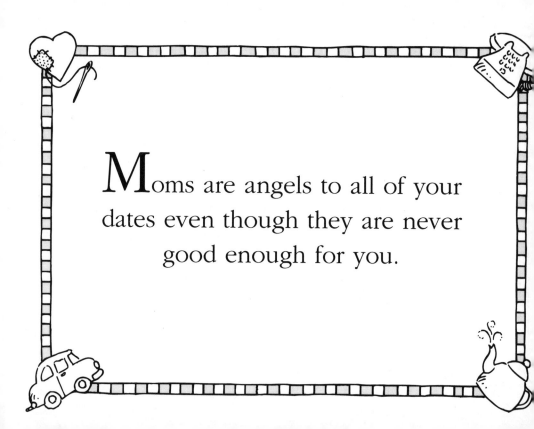

Moms are angels to all of your dates even though they are never good enough for you.

Moms are special angels who don't care what other mothers do.

Moms are special angels who ask questions with no answers.

Moms are angels who help you with new math, new shoes, and the new boy next door.

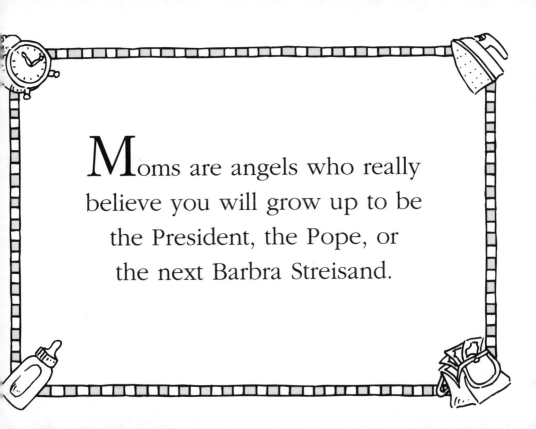

Moms are angels who really believe you will grow up to be the President, the Pope, or the next Barbra Streisand.

Angel moms never buy retail.

Moms are angels who carry extra tissues so you never have to use your sleeve.

Moms are angels with special
Band-Aids to mend broken toys,
broken dishes, and broken hearts.

Moms are angels who believe
you when you say there's a
monster in the closet.

Moms are angels with extra eyes
in the backs of their heads.

Moms are special angels who believe problems are growth experiences.

Moms are special angels who
love you after your divorce.

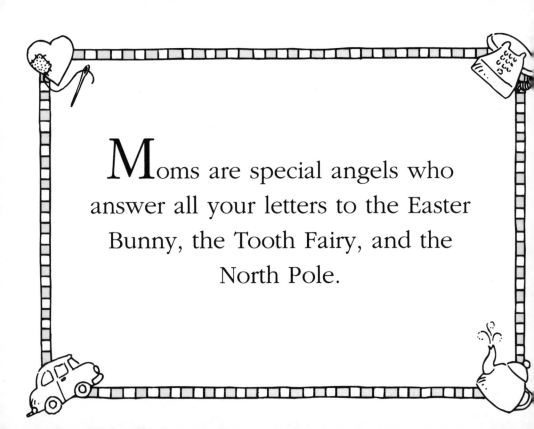

Moms are special angels who answer all your letters to the Easter Bunny, the Tooth Fairy, and the North Pole.

Moms are angels who lend you their beaded sweaters with shoulder pads, makeup, and high heels for dress up.

Moms are angels who never run out of oatmeal, hot chocolate, Jell-O, or chicken soup.

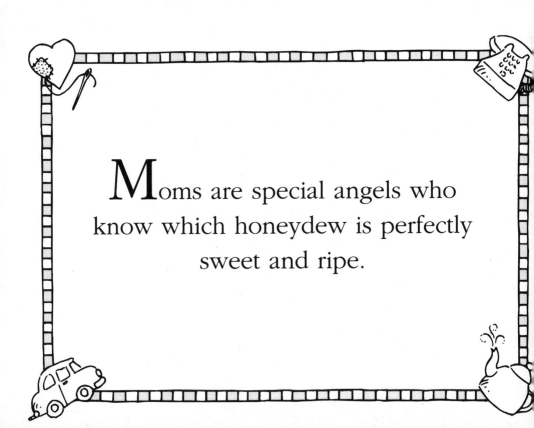

Moms are special angels who know which honeydew is perfectly sweet and ripe.

When in doubt, angel moms
wing it.

Moms are special angels who screen your phone calls when you're home and pretend to be your secretary when you're out.

Moms are special angels who teach you left from right, right from wrong, and always to send a thank you note the next day.

Moms are angels who patch up your teddy with pretty red hearts so the stuffing doesn't come through.

Angel moms always buy school clothes two sizes too big.

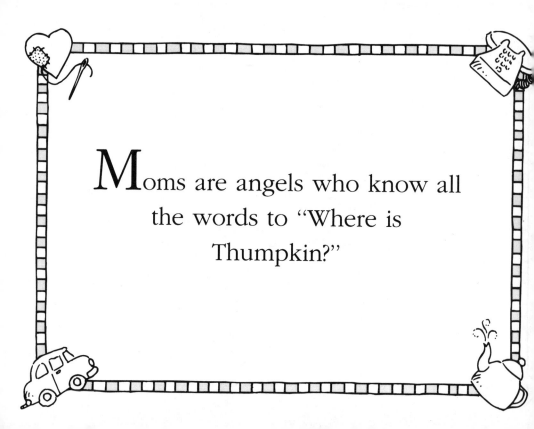

Moms are angels who know all the words to "Where is Thumpkin?"

Moms are special angels who never get tired of saying "Who's there?" when you say "Knock, knock."

Moms are special angels
who bring you ginger ale, toast,
and magazines when you don't feel
so well.

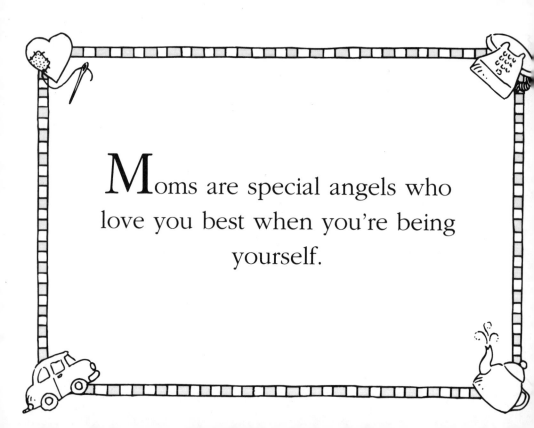

Moms are special angels who love you best when you're being yourself.

Angel moms teach us
grace under pressure.

Moms are special angels who give your fiancée the tray you made in Boy Scouts as an engagement gift.

Angel moms give their children roots of tradition, love, and wings of their own to fly.

Moms are special angels who keep the door wide open even after you leave home.

Moms are special angels who are your biggest fans.

You're never too old for a lullaby.

Home is where the heart is.

Moms are special angels who can't wait till you have children of your own.

Moms are special angels who coach you through your first dinner party.

Moms are special angels who ride in the front seat of the roller coaster even though they are scared silly.

Moms are angels with special radar to help you find your homework, your car keys, a prom dress—and yourself.

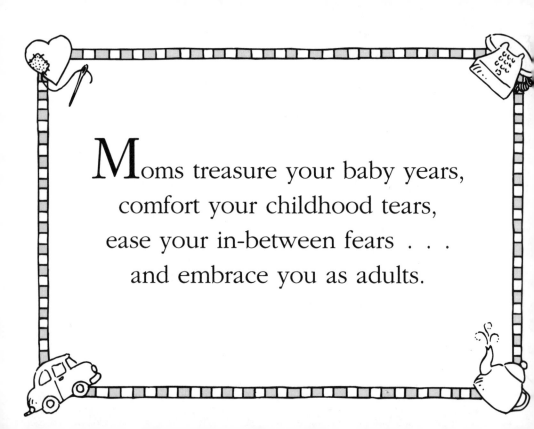

Moms treasure your baby years,
comfort your childhood tears,
ease your in-between fears . . .
and embrace you as adults.

You are never too old to be
tucked in at night.

Moms are special angels who lend you their wheels when yours are in the shop.

Mom is "your secret pal" when you need a friend.

Angel moms know how to juggle.

A mom's dictionary has "Maybe," "We'll see," and "Later" instead of "No."

Bragging is a mother's inalienable right.

Moms are special angels who remember the names of all of your boyfriends.

You can never have too many
magnets on the refrigerator.

One moment of love every day
adds up to a happy childhood.

You'll understand when you have children of your own.

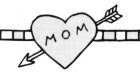

Moms are special angels who
turn "ughs" into "hugs."

Moms are angels with laugh lines, not wrinkles.

The terrible twos last from age 2 through 52. Then they're on their own.

You're never too old to bring
your laundry home.

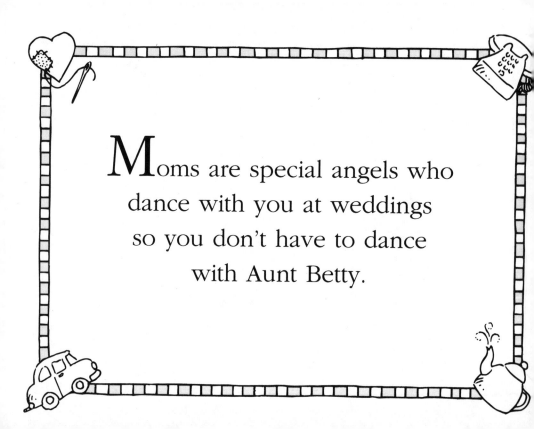

Moms are special angels who dance with you at weddings so you don't have to dance with Aunt Betty.

Moms are special angels who know how to get the stain out of your new blouse.

Moms are angels who pretend
they never wait up for you.

Moms are special angels who can read *Goodnight Moon* for the 405th time with meaning.

Moms are angels who can wait
until you thank them later.

Bonnie Altenhein was born and raised in New York City, and has been writing about everything from angels to zebras since she was old enough to hold a crayon. She was editor of *Better Homes and Gardens* magazine, former secretary and "joke coordinator" for Joan Rivers, and creator of WATCH MY LIPS!—a unique, million-dollar company that developed a line of "greeting seed" cards that became an overnight industry phenomenon. She has been featured in *Business Week, Advertising Age,* and other publications.

Nominated several times for the "Louie" award—the highest honor for greeting card writers, Ms. Altenhein is a free-lance writer/designer and the author of a bestselling calendar, poster, and several greeting cards featuring angels. Her previous books are *How Angels Get Their Wings, Christmas Angels,* and *Angel Love.*

Monica Sheehan has illustrated numerous books, including *How Angels Get Their Wings, Christmas Angels, Angel Love, The Toast Always Lands Jelly Side Down, Quotations to Cheer You Up When The World Is Getting You Down,* and *Dr. George Sheehan on Getting Fit and Feeling Great.* She lives on the Jersey shore.